Prepare To Se

A Handy Toolbox

For Sufferers of

Post-Traumatic Stress

A Survival Technique Not a Disorder

Eva C. Kretschmar

Prepare to Sense Demons

A Handy Toolbox

Post-Traumatic Stress

A Survival Technique

Not a Disorder

Medical Disclaimer: The following information is intended for general information purposes only. Any application of the material set forth in the following pages is at the reader's discretion and is his or her sole responsibility. For most traumatised individuals it's paramount to seek advice from a health care provider or work alongside the support from a therapist.

i

To Frank,
for support in my adolescence.

To my father,
for being my true mountain.

To Alice and Hannah,
for keeping me alive and safe.

To Mark,
for his unfaltering patience, compassion,
companionship and inspiration (from the red
chair).

To Billy Hoskins,
for design and editing of the book cover.

To my mentors and trauma specialists,
for their guidance, support and invaluable
contributions to my writing process.

A Handy Toolbox

Anyone who struggles to cope with life may benefit from the **10 Steps** in this handy toolbox, a little self-help book.

This little self-help book may empower you to find 'release and resolution' from traumatic experiences by reconnecting your presence of mind, body and spirit. Use it, not to fix your troubles, but embrace and process them. Just as an artist takes his brushes wherever he goes, you can take these STEPS along with you and use them when you feel overwhelmed by anxiety and worry. Let them be your toolbox, your resource, enabling you to implement these strategies at any moment providing support and guidance through life's challenging experiences.

This book can be read from beginning to end, or if you wish you can simply go straight into the **10 Steps**. Either way, enjoy your journey to greater ease, self- confidence and a connection with life that is truly settled and centred.

Any mentally, physically or chronically ill individual may benefit from the practices in this toolbox. Anyone suffering from OCD, ADHD, heart conditions, depression or the many more 'disorders' and 'illnesses' that we encounter in our world today, **can** learn to build a safe foundation from which to experience self-care, self-love and self-worth. This is the space from hence we learn to self-regulate and self-control. This is the space from hence changes in life emerge.

Contents

Prologue

Just like you I am scared, anxious, distressed in many situations.
But I manage, get by, and yet often wish for better.

It has been years, a long journey I fail to comprehend,
But have learned to have faith and be patient.

Be patient. Stop. Let life come to you.
Wait and discover moments of sadness and moments of joy - moments of impact that define who you truly are.

Scared, anxious, distressed but ok! When you realise that living life to the full is just that, and more,

Your whole life belongs to you.

Impacts

I've had my fair share of traumatic experiences. I've lived and struggled with, sensed and conquered demons, and now live contentedly alongside post- traumatic stress.

 When I was 11 years old I got hit by a lorry. I was on a horse. The lorry hit the horse. The horse saved my life. The horse died. I was gone for a while. Not connected. Detached; out of body; out of self.
 'An ambulance for a horse' the headline in the paper read. My frontal bone pressed on my brain. I had to have an operation. I have the scars to prove it.

When I was eighteen I had a car accident. Exceeding speed and losing control. Chopped down a hedge then smashed through a wall. The policeman offered a cigarette... I was in a daze; shock; dream. Not connected. Detached; out of body; out of self. As if someone had switched off the lights.

3

When I was twenty I was on a plane. We got hit by lightning. There was a flame. One engine failed. The plane started going down. People were holding hands. I started talking to God: 'Where are you taking us??'
I went out there, somewhere into the beyond. Detached; out of body; out of self.

I remember the tubes and barred windows in the hospital room. I was 11. I remember the tunnel filled with a bright light when the car spun out of control. I was 18. I remember the numbness and stillness when the plane went down, somewhere out of body, out of self; and the intense release of tears when my feet touched the ground again. Back inside my body, yet still disconnected with my Self. Confused and frightened. I was 20.

At the time I didn't recognise the effects of these traumatic experiences. I was in shock. Life felt numb, frozen and translucent.

Hereafter my body started to behave in very uncomfortable, stiff and chaotic ways every time I was faced with happenings and situations in life that asked of me to be myself. According to others I failed to cope. I wanted to cope and fit in, but seemed to have lost my footing. I had slipped off the trodden path. Life became too much, overwhelming. I was outside and couldn't get back to my own inner self. My body started to function and react awkwardly. Tension and stiffness started to build and anxiety and fear started to grow. The more uncomfortable, scared and unsafe I felt, the more I found a way to leave my body in order to find a place where I could cope, survive.

I withdrew from human contact. Though painful, it enabled me to feel myself. That pain of loneliness, not belonging felt real. I starved myself and that pain of hunger was real. Though a struggle for survival it gave me a sense of existing; a distorted way of belonging. I found ways to ease the pain and live alongside the fear of living. Going out of body into a space beyond, disconnected from reality, felt safe. I escaped from a detached fragmented life into a dream world which allowed me to cope. This survival technique kept me alive.

I would seek out quiet, open, deserted spaces where I could reconnect with my true self and be one with nature ; a space non-threatening with no demands or responsibilities. Here, where I felt safe, I could breathe and recover that sense of being truly alive. Yet the more frightened I became, the longer the process of coming back took.

These self-defining accidents, these moments of impact were the triggers. These experiences were a shock to my system. At the time I was not attentive and aware of these moments of impact. Their significance was incomprehensible.

My coping mechanisms were too fragile. I became insecure and mentally unstable. I escaped to a place where I felt safe, a sort of other-worldly dream reality. This pattern of existence became addictive. It became my survival technique. It became home. Doctors called it 'manic-depressive'. I was hospitalised, institutionalised for 4 months. Here I could scream, tremble, cry and shake without feeling guilty or ashamed.

I was held and heard as an adult, an equal, without regressing into being the 'inner child' hurt, frightened and vulnerable. I felt accepted for who I was. I felt safe.

But it didn't last. I wasn't able to carry that trust along with me into the real world. Though I was heard I wasn't given the tools to function and cope with life's demands and responsibilities. I wasn't given the steps paramount to enable me to be an adult with resolution and maturity to bear life. I may have released trauma in countless therapy sessions but hadn't come to resolution. Resolution is found in being able to live alongside the trauma and the realisation that the trauma is inside you; is you.

All therapies play a huge part in the psychosomatic process of growing in maturity, self-confidence and self-love. However without simple steps, tools, just like a new-born learns the first steps from a prime carer, life seen as normal by society is likely to prove overwhelming and becomes a means of getting by, or barely surviving.

My parents and friends were worried. I wasn't like everyone else, leading a normal life. The real world appeared difficult and overwhelming to breathe in. Trying to get me back to where I was too frightened to be only made it worse. I went where the horses go when they run free. Wild but connected. They are one with nature, mother earth. They flow in one long stride like water with tremendous strength, spirit and determination. Their feet are *in* the ground - one with body, breath, awareness. Alert but relaxed. Spirit and soul are one with the elements.
They understood. They kept me alive.

 A longing to belong made it agonisingly painful to be in the real world. Withdrawing into a world beyond became my reality. Here I felt safe, secure and good enough – a survival technique so brilliant, I came to depend on it. It became sickeningly addictive. It became real.

There are no answers here. I believe it is just the way life is. Some trees grow while others take root, wither and die.

Maybe we need to acknowledge that and realise that this is life's way of keeping balance.

What is the connection between life and death? Like two sides of a coin, one cannot exist without the other.
I figure they ask of us what we are not here for. In death we are not here for living, and in life we are not here for dying. So right now I am alive, so I am not dead.

What does it mean to be alive? Living is difficult most of the time; a struggle mostly. What does being truly alive feel like? Alert, relaxed, focused, connected, loving, and passionate, and being in tune with your true self through each vital moment. And where is this space? In belly, heart, just is, as I simply am.

So what does difficult mean? Not alive, all crunched and knotted up, disconnected, scared, rigid and chaotic. Stuck!
Where? Inside the head, like a compressed spring, unable to uncurl, release, let go or breathe.

You cannot sense the here and now. You are not yourself, but feel chased by demons. A sense of no release because you lost the connection and the world all around - same world as when alive - turns into a distant, isolated and fearful place. Reality becomes scary until it becomes unreal. Breath stops to flow and nurture your body. As you lose awareness you lose your body, your true self. The real world that is alive, free, beautiful and safe becomes demonic and overwhelming. Even the things we love become stressful. Body, breath, awareness are no longer one. You are not alive, yet living? Like two sides of a coin- life can be dying and death can be living.

Life's reality is always the same - a world of connection, balance and wholeness. Body, breath, awareness, One, simple but true.

So what is that place where you are all crunched up, scared, numb and filled with the feeling of non - belonging and no return?

The world is still the same reality. When inside the centre of our own circle, sphere of being, life is real, alive and beautiful. Here we pay attention. Here we are aware of reality's components and sense them for what they actually are.

When we lose our footing, step outside the centre of our own circle, we go off the path which bears life with all its aspects, and simply cannot see it for what it is. When our energies in motion (emotions) flip off balance, the real world becomes alien, scary and fearful.

As fear is self-created, the reality around us turns into a dramatic, even demonic space. Life feels tense, lost, confused, and even the simplest of tasks become difficult or even impossible to perform.

 The way to survive is by entering and existing in a world of belief rather than reality.
Once stuck in your head you are driven by emotions (thoughts, feelings, memories) which have gone off balance and become wound up, twisted until out of control.

Energy in motion gone awry leaves you feeling unsafe and worthless. You don't feel good enough. You survive by trusting disturbing thoughts and feelings which you believe are real and right. Body and head are disconnected.

The longer you push your body like a lorry the more you lose connection with your natural intelligence, your intuition and true sexuality. You lose your body, your true self, which is a finely tuned instrument.

So the more uncomfortable, stiff and chaotic you get in your body, the more you lose your true self. Your head, like a control centre, starts to be in charge of your behaviour and communication skills. Like an instrument coming out of tune. This is painful and difficult to be around, as well as painful to be.

So how can we stay here and be connected with the reality we live in? How can we be centred in our self (body, breath, awareness) rather than drifting, sinking into despondency and be eaten alive by our self-created demons?

Let us begin with a simple Tai Chi practice.

This may not be simple to begin with, but with perseverance you will soon connect with the practice and enjoy using it as a stabiliser in stressful moments or any situation that requires you to be calm and collected.

A Simple Practice

Imagine you are sitting (lying or standing) in the centre of your own circle.

Do not make it intense. Have fun. Be curious. Stay focused. Alert but relaxed.

Any thoughts that arise acknowledge them, imagine putting them in a box, shut the box and throw it out of the window, for now.

Slow down. Be patient with yourself. Remember you are a finely tuned instrument, not a lorry you can push about.

No matter where you are in the circle, it is OK!! Daily practice and focus on where you are in the circle will bring you into the centre.

Some days this is easier than others, but that is OK, because that is life's challenge.

Once you get the hang of this practice you can use it anywhere, particularly in situations that make you feel anxious and unsafe.

Your circle may be of any shape or form as long as it completely surrounds you. It may represent a bed of flowers, a warm pool of water or any space that you can relate to. It is your circle, your space! Make it as homely and comfortable as you can. Simply feel good and safe in it.

If you find it difficult to settle into this practice begin lying down before you practise it sitting or standing.

Make sure you are comfortable and warm. Just connecting with feeling comfortable may prove difficult if your mind is distressed and agitated. Patient endurance and going at your own pace is vital.

Make sure you turn phones off and settle in a room without a phone or other distractions in it. Commit to the time that you decide to do the practice in.

 Don't rush off elsewhere straight after to allow the benefits to filter through and help the mind unwind and settle. It's good to rest a little after the practice.

Practise daily (preferably 3 x 5 to 10 mins)

Appropriate Disorder

"There'll come a time when diseased condition will not be described as it is today by the physicians and psychologists but it'll be spoken of in musical terms, as one would speak of a piano that was out of tune."

Rudolph Steiner

I do not call you anything, label you or give you a name. I do not treat it as a disorder but recognise it as a great survival technique. I do not wish to take it away from you but support you in being able to come back into tune.

Being praised makes us feel good about ourselves. Equally, when we are told off we feel inadequate and not good enough.

So, if I were to tell a person that they have PTSD (post-traumatic stress disorder), or if I were to label them as 'mentally ill', they are likely to feel de- humanised.

They are forced to be their illness. They feel a sense of failure, a sense of being less than who they truly are.

There is a wealth of research and the signs that point to a person suffering from PTSD have been thoroughly examined: not sleeping, anxiety, panic attacks, and depression, self-harm, addictions ... where does the list begin and where does it end?

Is it not an insult to hand over some label to someone who is in (shell-) shock to tell them they have a disorder and that the condition will be suppressed through [often high dosage] medication?

A system already fragmented, lost and in turmoil, is drugged to shut down the symptoms. Surely if I'm already at screaming point I need help to release the demons, not stifle them.

Diagnosis can be problematic. The interpretation of symptoms is never consistent.

Outwardly, one person might be depressed yet still able to cope with life, while another, showing similar symptoms might struggle to function and believe they cannot function. I like to focus on how a person functions and responds physically, psychologically as well as spiritually.

'Prepare to Sense Demons' enables a person to reconnect with their true self and regain confidence to trust their intuitive voice: I feel good enough as I love and trust my body and soul, my Self.

What are these 'demons'?

They are horrific, scary, threatening, disturbing, unsettling and upsetting emotions that affect and turn us into fearful, anxious, distressed and dysfunctioning human beings.

Life is full of turmoil and torment, and the fear of living becomes worse than living itself. An experience affects us when we do not feel secure and safe. We cannot trust nor love ourselves. In order to cope and survive our whole system starts to react and disorientate. Our posture and body language become rigid and twisted. Our mental state, behaviour and communication and social skills become dysfunctional and distorted.

If we are unfortunate and do not have someone who can truly hold us and keep us safe, we will 'go off the rails'.

We lose our footing and begin to trust in this harmful and destructive behaviour, lose perspective and believe it to be right and real. We are conned by its demonic charm until it becomes addictive and normal.

As fear does not exist but is learned from impacts, our entire life becomes one of belief, not reality. The only fear that is real is the fear of falling.

When truly nourished and nurtured by the sadness and unconditional love of our Mother, we can face life with its experiences of dark and light as this is how real life is: scary yet beautiful; shocking yet welcoming; cruel yet caring; angry yet loving; confrontational yet passionate; disrespectful yet trusting; intrusive yet empathetic.

Our Mother refers to anything that truly and unconditionally loves and respects and believes in us. Anyone or anything that makes us belong, feel home, safe and alive.
This could be God, Faith, Mother Earth, a soul mate, parent or animal, a place or even an object.

To be truly free requires courage. This is a learning process which should ideally take place during our very first steps in life.

Yet often confusion, inconsistency and traumatic experiences get in the way. It means we have to relearn these steps later on in life to rediscover the freedom and truth of who 'I am'.

This is not research, not analysing, but just my story and my way of bearing life. From great therapists, family and friends through to self-healing, not because of one amazing treatment or technique, but a long process, a journey slow, tormented, painful but enriching with every step. The latter I'm only aware of now and realise is the reason so many people do not move on. They believe it is not working for them as they are still scared, stressed and not able to function in life. They believe life entitles them to be happy, look good and feel good. I figure the reality from which joy grows is often the opposite.

Let's be realistic the misery in our mind is what creates problems. In spite of people believing, even being convinced they cannot or should not have to bear this misery, this is not what real misery is.

A long road well worth travelling, though I can only see that now! The moments of impact, experiences in life that define who we are. This is one of those moments.

I still get frightened, scared and distressed, and I always will. That is part of the essence of life! But I do not have to escape into the beyond, go out of body, disappear or disconnect.

I am here now and scared, anxious or not, I've learned to say it is OK! I am loveable as I am. I've come home. Just because I'm different does not mean I'm ill.

So here are a few simple steps and guidelines which, if practised daily (!!!), will create shifts and changes in your life.

These steps won't fix your life but create a psychosomatic process which brings maturity and self-confidence. You learn to self-care and self-regulate which enables you to self-control.

Change towards the better? Yes, I like to think so. Just remember change can be towards the worse before it changes to the better.

This is often the most important part of your journey. The day will come that you realise the demons are your gateway to your true self.

Make sure you are in a safe space with someone you trust, or a therapist at the beginning of your practice, until you become aware, that though scary, it is ok to practise on your own, as you have learnt when to stop and stay in the here and now. These are basic steps which we should learn early on in our lives. Most of us didn't.

I will not tell you, you have a disorder or an illness as I believe this creates the illness. You are who you are with everything that you are. You are totally lovable, you just lost your path, your footing which is where your connection with and sense of self stems from.
When you lose your footing your existence becomes a dream, and life's happenings one of belief rather than reality.

This world of belief feeds on emotions (energy in motion off balance) that've been chasing you for a long time.

How about having a go at coming back to reality and learn to sense and sever the demons. Don't make it hard work. Be inquisitive, give it a shot and have some fun with it. Remember not to rush. This process is slow but lasting!

Before I begin I just like to voice that the ideas and practices in this little self-help book are from great teachers, friends, family and therapists along the way of my journey of coming back.
I am forever grateful for the support and would simply like to share what helped me find my way home, feeling good about myself despite my fears and anxieties.

I still have my ups and downs, moments of horror, fear and sadness, yet know that it is just so and that is ok!

It's the sensing of demons while in a safe and real space that enables us to sever from and befriend them to get on with life. We can embrace life living with the demons, but without them taking charge of our lives.

Using these 10 Steps as tools enables you to be more comfortable in your body and stay in the present moment, stress and worry free. Remember stress and worry might still be there but don't take control.

I always remind myself that the only place that matters is the present moment as that is all that is real. When we worry we grow fearful, and from fear we become distressed. It is self-created and causes us to lose the ability to choose a different way to the one we have become to believe to be true.

You might ask but how can I be comfortable in the here and now, if I can't bear to be in it? Can't bear to be here?

Have faith! Let's start right from the beginning. Don't rush to jump ahead until a practice is comfortable and you begin to practise it naturally. Make it part of your life, like brushing teeth. Just practise. Don't try, just have a go and observe. If the practice feels good, great, if it doesn't, well that's ok too. Just keep practising. It gets easier as you go along.

Without constant practice and reminders we stay arrested in our own thoughts, perceptions and opinions, restraining us from moving forward in the psychosomatic process of self-development. With time change happens and the practice itself enables us to experience how we have changed. Endure, surrender and trust in the simplicity of your practice. Though often difficult and in darkness, love, joy and light will reveal itself.

The 10 Steps

Step 1   Breathing

Sit or lie comfortably in a quiet space. Make sure you are warm.

Imagine your breath comes to you from a beautiful star in the distance, or a close friend or animal sends it to you. Then simply return the breath.

Focus on where the breath is coming from, not on the breath itself.

Practise daily 3 x 5-10 mins.

Step 2   A Dialogue

Relax into your breathing practice. (Step 1)

Now talk to your beautiful star, friend or animal. Ask 'how are you today?'

Then talk to the star about yourself: what you love doing; what you like about yourself; what you are good at and what you are not so good at; what you need and what you miss, or anything else you feel you need to get off your chest.

Practise daily regardless of how you feel. Do not rush. Think positively and sense what is important and necessary for you to share with the star. Do not question 'why'; simply be with your practice.

Practise daily 5-10 mins.

Step 3   A Simple Practice

Relax into your breathing practice. (Steps 1 & 2)

Now, do you remember 'A Simple Practice'?

Imagine you are lying (sitting or standing) in the centre of your own circle.

Relax into the sensation of where you are in your circle. Just pay attention, be aware and open-minded.

Don't be fascinated by anything that comes up. Simply observe. Stay as long as you wish. Don't rush to move on.

Practise daily 3x 5-10mins.

Step 4   Connect With Feet

Relax into 'A Simple Practice'.

Once settled in your circle, have a go at focusing on your feet.

Breathe from your feet.

Sense your in-breath moving up into your body, expanding and nourishing you, and then send it back down and out through your feet.

You may also try this from the outside tip of your vagina, penis or your belly button.

Pick the one that works for you!! As long as you stay with the one that feels right for you, it'll take you into a calmer, more grounded space.

A restless, agitated mind will be distressed by the slightest thing, whereas a calm and collected inner mental state enables you to see life clearly without unnecessary fascination, obsession or unnerving.

Be patient. Keep at it. Once you have got the hang of this practice use it in any situation that requires centring and calming.

Remember to practise it as often as is possible, so when faced with a stressful or unsettling situation you are able to connect and drop into the practice immediately.

Make the centre of your own circle your safe space. Feel free to take someone close to you into the circle with you, if that helps you feel safe.

Practise daily 3 x 5-10mins.

Well done so far! You might want to stay with these 4 Steps for a while so they can become rooted within your system. Once you feel confident in your practice move on.

Step 5 Check In

It is good to use Steps 1 to 4 as your warm up.

Once you feel relaxed and collected, practise 'Checking In' with the present moment.

 Look at the space you are in right now. What do you see? Check whether anything frightens or scares, or makes you feel unsafe. If there is anything that creates tension or anxiety remove it, that is, place it outside or remove you from it e.g. leave the room.

Practising 'Checking In' allows you to always find a way to feel safe. Make sure you look at things and see them for what they really are: e.g. a book is a book and just that! If it is red it is a red book and just that.

Don't let any emotional associations get in the way. Keep it real. Avoid the temptation of dwelling on thoughts or feelings that might arise. Endure the simplicity of staying in the moment as it presents itself. See clearly without the interference of any views or preferences.

If a practice is too overwhelming just stop. Say out loud: 'It is too much. I need some time out.'

Take as long as you need! The feeling of feeling safe will come but you have to practise seeing things for what they are and nothing else. Always voice when you need time out, as well as when you feel comfortable and ready to have another go.

In extremely traumatised cases this is a challenging process and would need the support of a trusted friend or therapist. Though this may seem an easy process to some, others may feel extremely overwhelmed by having to voice out loud what they need.

Self-regulation comes from self-care and is the stepping stone to self-control. People that feel not good enough, worthless, believe they don't deserve 'Time Out' and are scared to say 'No'. They know not what it means to set clear boundaries for fear of losing attention.

 Voicing is an extremely difficult part of the practice. Patient endurance and constancy in your practice will awaken your true voice and remove inhibitions, shame, guilt and blockages. Once the true voice reveals itself, the need for attention diminishes and your character and behaviour begin to change. Slowly you realise living gets easier and you feel more at peace.

Practise daily as often as possible.

Step 6 Inside My Body

Relax into your breathing practice and the centre of your own circle. 'Check In'. (Steps 1 to 5)

Now have a go at sensing where you are in your body? Do you sense yourself in all of your body or maybe just in one part like a foot, shoulder or in belly. Or maybe you sense where you are **not** in your body.

Be patient. Just have a go, and if it doesn't happen straight away, simply have another go the next day. There is no right or wrong here. Just be curious to and observe what you sense.

Practise daily 5 to 10 mins.

Step 7   Head Into Belly

Relax into your breathing practice. Settle into the centre of your own circle. 'Check In'. Sense whereabouts you are in your own body.
(Steps 1 to 6)

Part 1:

Now have a go at bringing your attention from inside your head down into your belly. Imagine you swim, walk, ride or in any way that is comfortable for you, down a midline, like a lane or path, until you feel yourself drop into your belly.

By belly I mean below the belly button, as though into the bowl of the pelvis where we belong and our true intelligence, being and sexuality come from.

49

Go slowly. If difficult, take a friend, animal or object along with you.
Have a sense of moving or sliding down a midline. This can feel very uncomfortable, sad, scary, even upsetting and unsettling. It is OK! Though difficult it gets easier with practice. Be patient.

You CAN STOP at any time and start again tomorrow. If possible stay with it even if just for a short while, but DO NOT let yourself get to the space where it feels too much. Remember TIME OUT!!

You can back up at any point in the practice, and then slowly move further down. It might be helpful to practise this with someone for support in the beginning.

Remember stay in the present moment, keep 'checking in' and always feel safe!! Only if you feel ready and are still able to focus add **Part 2.** Otherwise stop now! Well done!

Part 2:

Once you enjoy coming and settling into your belly, have a go at sensing how old you sense yourself in your belly. Maybe you get a sense of yourself when you were a child, as well as sensing yourself at the age that you are now. Take a look at how the two of you relate to one another. If you feel happy hugging or holding each other's hands, go ahead. You might even be able to look into each other's eyes.

Sometimes you might even get a sense of a higher self, a sense of a presence that is you who knows exactly who you are and want to be. Perhaps all three selves: child, you and higher self might enjoy holding one another. Take a look and if there is no such connection do not worry. One day you'll feel something.

Practise daily for 10 mins. Build it up once you feel comfortable.

Step 8   Midline

Relax into your breathing practice. Settle into the centre of your own circle. 'Check In' and move your attention into your belly.
(Steps 1 to 7)

Now see if you sense a midline in your body. Imagine a vertical line right down the centre (crown to coccyx) of your body. Have a go at breathing in and up your midline, then down and out when you exhale. Imagine your in-breath travelling from the tip of your coccyx right up to the crown, and your exhalation travelling from the crown back down to the coccyx.

Stay focused and anchored in your belly during this practice, and do not lose the centre of your own circle.

Well done! Just enjoy the sensation 'I am in my belly; I breathe from my coccyx to my crown and from my crown back down to my coccyx.' With practice you will connect with your midline like a pendulum swing. You begin to organically connect with the rhythm of your being as part of this life.

When you organically connect and sense yourself dropping into stillness as if dropped down to the bed of the ocean or deep into a field full of wild flowers, have a go at sensing your breath coming up through the soles of your feet. Feel it move up and connect with the midline (feet, coccyx to crown), then all the way back down (crown to coccyx, feet).As though your feet were your nose. Enjoy the sense of breath nurturing your whole being.

Build up slowly! Always return to the previous practice if it is too much, until it feels part of you. It is you. Never push! Never rush!

If 10 mins is too much start with less and slowly build it up!!

Life around us is fast and furious, so it is often difficult to trust slow and safe!!

The more you slow down, the more connected with yourself and the ground you will become, and be able to overcome obstacles.

Always practise in a quiet and safe space!!

Practise daily 10 mins. Build up to 30 mins.

Step 9   Q & A

By now Steps 1 to 8 should feel part of your daily life, a bit like brushing teeth. You just do it! You might find Steps 1 to 8 have helped you feel less anxious, more centred, confident, connected and grounded.

Feel free to pick any step you particularly enjoy and practise it on its own or keep up all the steps, as long as you keep at it every day.

If the odd day you don't manage acknowledge this and simply return with diligence.

The next step takes a bit more resolve and commitment. But remember, life is not easy and moments of joy derive from working through, facing and being with challenging spaces and experiences.

Let us have a go!

Get yourself a notebook. Hardback A5 is best.

Write down the question:' What do I feel in my belly?' or 'How do I feel in my belly?' Pick the question that works for you! Now jot down whatever you sense in your belly. You have **3** seconds to jot down the answer. Whatever comes up, write or put it down. If nothing comes up put 'nothing' or leave it blank.
Only jot down what you sense, not the reason 'why' you sense it .You may draw or scribble the answer if that is what comes up.

Example:

Question: 'What do I feel in my belly?'

Answer: 'Nothing' / 'Stones rumbling'/ 'hot feet'/ 'horses galloping'/ 'wriggling'…

Or

Example:

Question: 'How do I feel in my belly?'

Answer: 'pissed off'/ 'in a muddle'/ 'lost'/ 'like broken bones'...

Practise daily for 2 weeks. Always write the question, and then within **3** seconds write the answer.

I want you to hear the voice (true voice) in your belly, not the analytical voice from your head. It will reveal itself in time. You will know when it happens as it has an innate, organic, even orgasmic sense, sigh or groan to it.

Make a note of date and time for each entry.

Step 10 On Reflection

Firstly repeat Step 9.

Now add: 'What is good about this?' and 'What is bad about this?' Remember only **3** seconds to answer each question. When you have answered all the questions begin your final sentence with 'On reflection I realise ...' and finish it within **3** seconds.

Example:

'What do I feel in my belly?'
'I feel stones.'

'What is good about that?'
'I can hear it rumbling.'

'What is bad about this?'
'I'm lost.'

'On reflection I realise that I miss home.'

Or

Example:

'How do I feel in my belly?'
'Uncomfortable.'

'What is good about that?'
'I am aware of it.'

'What is bad about that?'
'I don't know what to do with it.'

'On reflection I realise that I need to slow down.'

Remember to do this **once** every day. You will find your way with it. It helps you develop greater self- awareness.

Once you have got the hang of this reflective questioning and answering, you may then ask any starter question - as long as you begin the question with 'What' or 'How', never ask 'Why'!!!

Anything you like to find out about yourself e.g. 'What do I worry about?'; 'How come I feel anxious?'; 'What makes me fearful?' or 'What makes me happy?'; 'How have I become joyful?' or 'What has made me sad?', 'How does my heart feel today?'...

Ask any question you feel would help you understand how you are at this present moment.

Revision

Awareness

Our life experiences depend on how we focus. When focused we can pay attention to the steps that we take. This creates awareness and enables us to slow down. This creates a process that allows for growth and maturity of our higher brain enabling us to 'stop before we act'.

When we are not in focus we behave in often irrational, over-excited, inattentive and unrealistic ways. Our nervous system turns irritable and chaotic. In turn life becomes off centre, unbalanced and we waste unnecessary energy. We lose the ability to pay attention and focus. Our behaviour and communication skills become impaired and we turn into dysfunctional human beings who are disorientated, disconnected, anxious, worried, stressed and even panic stricken. Our mental and physical state becomes unstable, rigid, destructive and eventually dis-ordered or 'ill'.

Demons, like fairies, angels or spirits, are everywhere. When life disarrays demons take charge and life turns into a bad dream, nightmare; trauma (German word for dream is Traum).

The madness of it is that the person afflicted believes this is the reality of life and hence becomes more discordant.

Good needs bad and bad needs good. This is an extremely important part of existence as it creates balance in life. When this balance loses its equilibrium we turn into self-obsessive beings driven by what we believe to be right (head, analytical) rather than what is true (belly, intuitive).

This is a challenging part of living to bear, yet paramount if change needs to take place.

Life has many faces yet the most difficult is being responsible for the bearing of once own life.

Do not avoid or suppress sadness or hardship but pay attention to it.

Let greater awareness bring joy and stillness.

Learn to 'STOP BEFORE YOU ACT!'

The **10 Steps** may help you on your way.

Give the **10 Steps** a go and commit to daily practice.

Make these **10 Steps** your tool box, a resource that you can take along with you whenever and wherever you need support to get through a situation. They may help you compose yourself and come back to wholeness and stay in balance.

The more you practise to focus and connect with your inner mental state the more relaxed, calm and centred you will feel. This enables you to pay attention and 'stop before you act.'

It is important to seek support and guidance when life has become too difficult to bear. We all go wrong, err, become anxious, worry, panic and create defensive yet detrimental and often destructive, harmful behavioural habits.
 These get us through life by avoiding the demons (the real issues) and tricking ourselves into believing this behaviour is right. Make belief becomes our existence.

As a reminder it is helpful to practise these steps with a trusted friend or a therapist, particularly when there is a history of trauma, mental issues, stress and depression. This ensures that you get helpful and constructive support during your practice, as well as someone holding you when it all gets too much.

We can all learn to accept our 'problems' and realise that they are not real issues but part of who we have become. As we mature and change in opinions and character, we enter stillness, acceptance, awareness, learn to reflect and realise that it is possible to live life to the full with all its sorrow and joy.

We all have to pay attention to experience what it means to live life to the full. Who said it was going to be easy?! Not easy but effortless when we stay aware through paying attention.

Be prepared that you may find this process difficult. It may be painful at times and you may be tempted to give up. Persevere – it's worth it!

Have a little faith. Trust in you and take time, when you can, to acknowledge what you have achieved so far. You will have moved on from who you used to be. Don't be too hard on yourself. Be kind on you.

It is important to be in a non-threatening space when you practise. If you are with someone, make sure they are someone with whom you feel comfortable and relaxed.
Like learning to play a musical instrument or ride a bike, keep up regular manageable spells of practice.

There will be days when you feel you have made progress; there will be days when you feel the opposite. There will be days when, for one reason or another, everything seems to fall into place. How or why this happened you cannot tell but that moment is a moment of impact that defines who you truly are.

Enjoy, have fun and do not make it intense. Take joy in coming back slowly. This process is slow but lasting. Not a quick fix, but a supportive foundation for life. Come back to simply being you:

'I breathe
I am in my feet
I am my feet
I am alive
I am.'

If you ever feel as though you are not making progress (this may happen at times and this is fine; the path is not always a smooth one), you might like to have a go at this gentle and easy meditation: **Easy SOS Practice**.

Easy SOS Practice

Lay your left hand, palm up, inside your right palm (right hand inside left might feel better for you). Now, imagine a bowl with no bottom. Place any thoughts that race through your head inside the bowl and simply 'flush' them down and away. Maintain this process and sense yourself dropping into a calmer, inner mental state. Now imagine your feet are in the ground. Sense your breath coming from a space about a meter down below, and feel yourself come back to greater awareness and stillness.

Like many things, it takes practise to master but has an immediate effect. It brings back the organic sense of being - alert but relaxed.

This is an easy SOS practice that enables you to stay focused rather than lose yourself to a torrent of thoughts, emotions and memories driving you along creating sheer overwhelm. You should not consider this to be an illness or a failing but simply a state of disorientation in which your connection with who you are is lost: being you, real, and experiencing life as such.

You are here. You made it, survived. You are loveable and wonderful as you are. You just need to take the steps to feeling good enough.

Have faith in you. Rediscover your true self – body, breath and awareness one. Find those moments of impact that define who you truly are. Enjoy greater awareness through sensing and paying attention. I am there right alongside you. Just shout if you need support.

Remember life is a struggle and hard work as it requires endurance, diligence, effort and focus to reap its rewards.

If ever a situation proves too challenging quickly move your body in any way possible.

For example take a few steps, slap your thigh, squeeze your cheeks, reach for a cup or open a window… It doesn't matter how you move as long as you simply MOVE!! This prevents your body from going into the 'freeze' stage where your system feels immobilised and completely arrested in its learned reactive behaviour pattern –frozen, stuck, dysfunctional and toxic.

Avoid the temptation wanting to rationalise or question 'Why am I doing these steps?' There is neither a need nor a point in analysing or understanding its meaning. What matters is diligent practice even though this may prove difficult, testing and challenging. As you commit to daily practice shifts and changes slowly begin to take place, often without you even being conscious of this. Others are likely to notice differences in you before you do yourself. Subtle changes occur which bring greater awareness and understanding of yourself and your emotions without you even having to try.

All you have to do is have a go, commit, be willing and have faith. Joy will derive from the practice and thenceforth the practice will be joyful.

Changes come to those that go about their practice daily and diligently. Those that constantly search for answers, proof and look elsewhere for that special treatment or therapy that will fix them may not reap the same benefits.

As nature has a way of righting itself when left alone, if we don't interfere but simply go about these steps, life will come 'right'. Remember 'right' means it is ok to be sad just as it is ok to be joyful. Having the tools to be OK with either turns the demons into your best friend and greatest teacher.

You may have been stuck with a chronic disorder or illness for years, and keep searching for that pill or therapy that will free, sever and release you from it.

But it is the disorder or illness that keeps you alive. It's a brilliant, though not necessarily pleasant, survival technique. Without it you might no longer be alive as you may not be able to bear life.

Prepare to sense demons and recognise them for what they are - a devilish cover up for who you really are but cannot trust yourself to be, through fear of the shame ridden 'inner child'.

This handy toolbox enables you to reconnect and release the child within and grow into the adult that you can truly be, and deep within the belly you know you already are.

Overcoming obstacles means recognising that the adult or child, that I'm now is not to be confused with the 'inner child' which bears the hurt and pain from experiences long ago. As we surrender the 'inner child' yearning for love and attention, true self emerges and grows in maturity, self- love and respect. Once the Self trusts its true voice a person feels secure and as an equal in the presence of others and towards him or herself.

Reminders

- Repairing and healing the body (you) is not instant. It requires acknowledgement, endurance and patience.

- Pain though not nice and often scary, is the body's way of telling you to slow down, stop doing and pay attention.

- Do not seek to ask a lot of questions or look for answers. Be content to observe and practise.

- Life is not one of routine, control or security. It is full of confusion, curiosity, intuition, ambiguity, courage and taking risks.

- Living is about recognising wrong turns for being the stepping stones to greater awareness and maturity.

- Pay attention, sense and trust your rhythm, keep a perspective and have a plan.

- Surround yourself with energies that accept you for who you are and challenge you passionately, instead of feeling sorry for you.

- Others feeling sorry for you, or feeling sorry for yourself will keep you traumatised. (This goes for humans and animals alike)

- Analysing (in the head) will only get you so far; practice and intuition (in the belly and heart) will get you home.

- Trust the innate wisdom that already bears your true voice (true intelligence).

- Practise with diligence and endurance.

- Observe, practise, be playful, curious and with open heart, and true intelligence naturally follows.

- NEVER hesitate to seek support or ask for 'TIME OUT'. It is ok to say 'No'!

- Be content with simplicity and attentive to the present moment.

- Surrender your beliefs and endure your Self.

- A calm and centred mind sees life for what it truly is.

- A distressed state of mind creates accidents, addictions, injury, pain, disorder and illness.

- **You** are loveable as **you** are!

Reflection

Nurture me so I learn to self-care.
Hold me so I learn to self-regulate.
When I feel safe I can self-control.

In the centre of my own circle I have courage to
be free.
In spite of many experiences that define who I
am,
I can learn to acquire a still mind, peaceful heart
and relaxed body.

A slow process, long journey, yet worthwhile to
help me belong,
Come home and be true to my Self.

I am good enough. I am home.

Acknowledgements

My gratitude goes to the minds that inspired and challenged me on my journey and encouraged me to find my voice by taking the steps that brought me home.

There are many great writers from Peter Levine; Daniel J. Siegel; Bessel A. van der Kolk ; David Emerson; Francine Shapiro; Eugene T. Gendlin; John Powell; Ajahn Chah; Andrew Still; John E. Upledger; Moshe Feldenkrais; Karen Horney; Eric Pearl; Hugh Milne; Rudolph Steiner; Tarthang Tultu; Stephen W. Porgess; Kenneth S. Cohen; Paul Grilley; Linda Hartley; Caroline Myss; John Bradshaw; Ida P. Rolf; Eric Franklin.....and many more without whose incredible insight and respect for the human spirit I could not have accomplished this work.

I would also like to thank the many therapists and friends who over the years have helped lay the stepping stones and given me the courage to walk with my feet *in* the ground.

About the Author

 Eva works in Surrey as a Registered Craniosacral Therapist, Reiki Master/Teacher, and a Movement Therapist ('Synchronicity through Yoga', and 'Feldenkrais Integrated Pilates'). Eva specialises in PTSD and Psychological, Physical and Behavioural Concerns. Eva also works as an Equine Reiki Therapist. She is a fully qualified secondary school teacher holding a Postgraduate Certificate in Education (PGCE). She offers workshops for teachers and pupils to support behavioural and mental issues in the education sector as well as offering workshops on 'Self-Healing' and 'Wellbeing' to the general public. For more information go to www.actevawellbeing.com

Printed in Great Britain
by Amazon

47699192R00061